THE LITTLE OFFICE OF THE
IMMACULATE CONCEPTION

MARTHA SILANO

saturnalia books

Saturnalia Books
105 Woodside Rd.
Ardmore, PA 19003
info@saturnaliabooks.com

ISBN: 978-0-9818591-9-4
Library of Congress Control Number: 2010939374

Book Design by Saturnalia Books

Cover Art: *Planetary* by Felicia Piacentino

Author Photo: Langdon Cook

Distributed by:
University Press of New England
1 Court Street
Lebanon, NH 03766
800-421-1561

Gratitude and thanks to the editors of the following publications in which these poems first appeared, some in slightly different versions:

32poems: "Poem After Vallejo"; *42opus*: "Your Laundry on the Line Like a Giant, Breathing Beast," "Way Over There"; *American Poetry Review*: "This is Not a Lullaby," "In Praise of Not Getting," "Ode to Imagination," "Easter Visit"; Anti-: "Her Panel"; *Babel Fruit*: "She Had Some Tantrums," "Shall I Compare Thee to a Spring Day at the Naples Zoo?"; *Beloit Poetry Journal*: "Where's Our Dignity?"; *Canary*: "No Refunds, No Exchanges"; *The Cincinnati Review*: "Love," "It's All Gravy"; *Crab Creek Review*: "Women Are Not Alone and That," "That Spring a Room Appeared"; Crab Orchard Review: "How to Sew"; *Cranky*: "The Norm Has a Standard Deviation of Plus or Minus Eleven"; *Columbia Poetry Review*: "Report from Connecticut on the Letter M, the AB Pattern, the Counting by 2s, 3s, and 4s"; *Escape Into Life*: "Made Pure by Her Intercession"; *Green Mountains Review*: "What I Will Tell the Aliens"; *The Journal*: "The Little Office of the Immaculate Conception," "More Waves May Follow," "I Live on Milk Street"; *New Orleans Review*: "Geography Lesson"; *No Tell Motel*: "My Place in the Universe," "Hate," "Thankful Quite Thankful," "Ten Days in Arkansas"; *Poetry Northwest*: "All Things Want to Float," "Ours"; *Prairie Schooner*: "Emergency Comfort Kit"; *Puerto del Sol*: "Santiago Says"; *Rhino*: "After Reading there Might be an Infinite Number of Dimensions"; *River Styx*: "What Are You Reading?"; *The Southeast Review*: "You're like the mean man"; *Tarpaulin Sky*: "Regrets Only, Please"; *TriQuarterly*: "This Parenting Thing," "I Wanted to Be Hip"; *Valparaiso Poetry Review*: "Because I Knew."

"Geography Lesson" is available online at *Poemeleon* (http://www.poemeleon.org)

Printed in Canada

Thanks to the editors at *The Journal* for nominating "I Live on Milk Street" for a Pushcart Prize, and the editors at *No Tell Motel* for nominating "Ten Days in Arkansas" for a Pushcart Prize.

"Love" is reprinted in *The Best American Poetry 2009*, edited by David Wagoner, series editor David Lehman (Scribner).

The author deeply and graciously thanks Kelli Russell Agodon, Susan Blackwell Ramsey, Stacey Luftig, Molly Tenenbaum, Moira Linehan Ounjian, Jenifer Lawrence Browne, and Lana Hechtman Ayers for their support, smarts, candor, and editorial prowess.

Hats off to the Rubies: Shannon Borg, Anna Maria Hong, Rebecca Hoogs, Erin Malone, and Kary Wayson.

Bushels of thanks to Arielle Greenberg.

A heaping bowl of gratitude to Michael Heffernan for his support, encouragement, and suggestion I make a visit to Roswell.

This book could not have been completed without the financial support of the following institutions:

The Boyden Family/Margery Davis Boyden Wilderness Writing Fellowship
The Helen Riaboff Whiteley Center
Washington State Artist Trust
Seattle 4Culture

I am grateful to Henry Israeli, editor of Saturnalia Books, for his patience and expertise, and to Campbell McGrath for choosing this manuscript for publication.

The daughter of the physicist thanks the father of the poet, Dr. Alfred A. Silano, for the countless pep talks and limitless, loving encouragement. Without him I could not have forged the trail down the astrophysics path: my gratitude and appreciation are boundless.

Daughter #2 thanks Delores Marie Victoria Katrosh Silano, aka Mother of Peace, for her sustaining and ever-present love and support.

TABLE OF CONTENTS

This book is for Riley and Ruby—the breath and shimmer in every poem,
and for Langdon, my Polaris.

WHAT I WILL TELL THE ALIENS

MY PLACE IN THE UNIVERSE

I think I am here
to stare carefully at maps,

then get lost at least fifty times a year.
I think I am here

to be suddenly
made aware of the loudness

of a ticking clock,
also to witness, in unexpected places,

glitter,
to hear a lady in heels

walking assertively down a hall.
The universe and I,

we're both expanding our knowledge
of what's just beyond us.

Me-n-the universe
really not separate after all,

me surely not a subset.
Me, the chairs, all

the couches, every soda can,
every book and eyelash,

all together making a music
unfortunately no one can hear

on account of the humming exhaust fans,
on account of the humming lights.

I LIVE ON MILK STREET

Via Lactea, to be exact. Once it was the path
to Zeus's palace, then a creamy cul de sac; now

they just keep widening and widening. Its origin?
On that the jury's still out. It could have been paved

by the Holy People who crawled to the surface
through a hollow reed, then formed my kind

from ears of white and yellow corn. Some say
it was born of Juno's wrath, wrath that tore

her breast from a suckling infant Hercules
(her no-good hubby once again knocking up

a mortal). What spurted up, they tell me,
begat this little avenue, this broad and ample road

where I merry-go-round with my 200-300
billion neighbors, give or take a billion or two.

(Then again, it might've all been cooked up
by Raven.) My street has the mass

of a trillion suns; my roundabout's a black hole.
My backyard abuts with my dear friend Io's.

She's always asking me to come on over,
but enduring speeds upward of 106,000 mph

usually means I'm waving from the porch.
(On the plus side, the ash from her many volcanoes

does wonders for my whispering bells.) I do wish
I could get to know the Leptons, though.

I invite them to my cookouts, but they're off
to hither and yon. And I don't mean to be catty,

but it's high time Ms. Nuclear Bulge
ponied up for some high power Spanx.

I know there's a whole lot else out there—
starbursts, whirlpools, Magellanic Clouds—

but I'm busy enough keeping up
with the slugs attacking my pole beans,

making sure the garbage goes out. Truth be told, I'm happy
right here where I am, lulled by my own sweet byway's

hazy halo, its harmony of traffic.

OURS

contains the ripping-metal croak
of a wader who eats its prey whole;
also a frog resembling a leaf, the male's
throat stuffed with its tadpole young;
we have tapeworms that latch
to intestinal walls, each segment self-
replicating. I guess we're all about making
more. And Styrofoam. And toilet paper.
We take pictures of empty parking lots
to show that sometimes they want us straight,
and sometimes they want us diagonal. Sculpt
from wood a human head, a headscarf
shrouding it, but stop me, I hardly know you.
          Okay, if you insist. We have pancreatic juices,
Extreme Shampoo for the dead cells shooting
from our non-wooden heads, and we have music,
magnetism, and dreams. We can drive forever
past nothing but wheat or corn, but then Mumbai,
22,000 people per square mile. Do you have
hobbies? Our favorite's folding paper into cranes;
we also love horses, and wiping each other out.
Our creation myth? A pool of acid and sugar
walked into a cave, began to paint on walls.
Has anyone mentioned fear?
          Where am I going? *Crazy. Wanna come?*
as my mom used to say, which is replication; mostly,
as I've said, what we do. We believe in money,
random mutation, though greed screws up everything.
But that Calder in Michigan—*La Grand Vitesse?*—
that's the kind of upward mobility we all can relate to.
          We pilate; we retreat, heal ulcers
with maggots; we nudist colony, vanilla
to Cozahome till wakened by a child's *who made
this world?* We'd like to be kissed and kissed
by a good kisser, touched and loved in a shade
of lipstick that becomes us. Invent new names
for cities and birds. To carry our young like a leaf-
like frog. Our world is an oven; we are the temperature.

OTHERS

1. Pancake

We like our batter fluffy, so we sift.
Whole-wheat vs. white? So pre-Big Bang.
There's an aura all around us,
yet nobody flips.

2. Sombrero

It might be a lot to get your head around,
but the black hole inside this crown is a billion times
the mass of your sun. Large as we are, we admire
your string of campfires guiding the departed toward Valhalla.

3. Exclamation Point

It's true! We're elongated! A rectangle aimed NW
at Mag 9! Aka the dot! With pulses of nebulosity!
Worth your time to find!

4. Taffy

There's a bridge between two of us resembling
those stretching bands of sticky goo
from deepest Jersey. Fralinger's famous—
Peach, Strawberry, Molasses Mint.
Craps schmaps. We prefer it here, pulling
and snapping while you lose your shirt playing slots.

5. Apple Core

Dim and distant—900 light years from where you hail,
we pride ourselves on heirlooms—Liberty, Spartan, Pink Pearl.
Winesaps and Wickson Crabs. Your biggest mistake? Letting
the Arkansas Beauty and the Tuscaloosa disappear.
This one? Gnawed on by a giant blue mouth,

then tossed out here, the farthest star in what
your kind call Cygnus.

6. Hamburger

Just be glad you're good and far away,
cuz the shit going down in this burg
makes your Agnes and Ike look like sun showers.
What happened first was a giant collision—imagine
a bacon and cheese slamming into a Coney.
The bacon went flying, while the mustard,
super-heated, shot out the opposite ends
at the speed of light. So now our bun's
got these spinning, spewing, fiery jets.
It's a mess! Not enough napkins to clean it up,
and no order of Mountain Dew to douse it.

7. Vacuum Cleaner

55 million light years away and receding briskly
from your dirty carpets and floors. Sometimes
it feels we were put here to mock you—us
and the folks who live in the Maytag. Cleaning,
and the loathing of it: maybe it's the true leveler,
our common ground. Let's strike a deal: we'll stop
the guilt-tripping if you stop sending spaceships
to places you don't need to go. Spend your money
cleaning up your own galaxy! (How's that
for a bunch of hot air?)

8. Tarantula

I know these guys give you the creeps,
but most of their sting is myth (no worse
than a bee's). Ours towers the ones that scuttle up
your Escalante Staircase. Good thing we're far
from your peeling front door, or else

we'd be casting shadows all over
your milky-white ass.

9. Footprint

That's right, a genuine I-was-here.
Judging by your passion for carving graffiti
into aspens, for re-reruns of *Planet of the Apes*,
you'd fit right in.

10. Dark Doodad

A long brown ribbon of doo-hickey,
like the ribbon of tongue hanging
from your don't-know-doodly-squat
mouth. If you've come here expecting
reassurances, you're in the wrong place.
Here we teach graveyard. Here our favorite language
is the one most dead.

WHAT I WILL TELL THE ALIENS

I will tell them about our clapping,
our odometers, and our skillets.

I will take them to a place of fierce
lightning, to a place of tombstones

and of gridlock, and I will tell them
of geckos, of ecstatic moments,

all about our tchotchkes, our temples,
our granite-countered kitchens.

Give me an alien and I will give it
a story of unfathomable odds,

of erections and looting. Show me
an alien and I will show it the sorrows

of the centuries, all wrapped up
in a kerchief, all wrapped up

in a grandmother's black wool coat.
Bring me an alien right now,

and I will show it the misery
of stilettos, of pounding out

tortillas and gyros. Please—
send me an alien, and I will give it

a bloody nose, and then I will show it a great
humanitarian gesture, 10,000 tents

when 600,000 are needed. Let me
talk to these aliens about shoe-shiners

and rapture, of holidays and faxes;
let me pray with the aliens for the ice

to stop melting, for the growths to stop
growing, for a gleam to remain on our lips

long after the last greasy French fry is gone.

IN MY BELLY

In my belly there is furniture—sofas
of satiny cowhide, tables of chicken wing
wood; in my belly the leather, boiled until softened,

chewed and swallowed because the man of the house:
Mother, bring me that Louis XV Pompadour; if we eat it,
we'll live another week. In my belly the stones

of Eritrean women, the ones they strap to their bellies
to quell the incessant grumbling; also the stones
placed each night in a pot of boiling water

when there is nothing, nothing, nothing. In my belly
the flying shrimp of Mozambique. In my belly the voice
of Adelesi Faisoni, who told me *there is no way to get used to hunger.*

In my belly the grains gathered by termites, retrieved
by humans, eaten with gusto despite the risk
of fatal allergic reactions. In my belly the lentil

that slowly destroys the central nervous system.
Here are the skin and the bones after the vultures
have left them. Here is every animal

in the Monrovia Zoo, excepting the one-eyed lion;
in my belly there is no one-eyed lion, very few
humans, very few items found at a typical

Food Lion–Tombstone Quick Bake Pepperoni,
Lean Cuisine. In my belly the pins the starving use
to extract the tiny kernels from marula fruit,

in my belly the skewers of roasted mice. And in my belly
there are cookies, cookies made of shortening, salt,
and mud. Mountains and mountains of beautiful

swirling cakes made of Haitian dirt. My belly is always
moving, moving and searching for locusts
that are shrimp, for leather that is lamb,

for the pot that boils while the children wait
and wait. In my belly the shouts of the giddy,
of the grateful for insects emerging, for the rolling boil

that lolls them. For how could their mothers,
with their steaming not-quite-done,
with their reassuring smiles, be lying?

IN PRAISE OF NOT GETTING

What time is it when an elephant sits on a fence?
Time for the chicken to wander lonely as a road, time

for the full-fledged conniption fit about what's not
on the fence or the road—*not that pink one! The other*

pink one! The one with the blue balloon on its rump,
the one she's grown fond of, used to, the one to grow on,

grown on, drone on, which is what time it is, and what makes it
so special? And he says sparkles, but I say a story I can't quite

figure out. I say, we need a verb: to art! To take the ho hum mundane,
and sparkle-ize it. Catch my glittery drift? Mine glimmering eye?

As in degree of usefulness. As in what the eye wants. Like billboards
salivating the dollar burger. Yes, we laughed when we saw the one

about the unibrow, but then we bought the ticket, bought it like the functions
of light and dark—sun equals crops, darkness tucks us into bed—

vs. all things good and bad. And also it's tidying. Sensing there's a mess,
making sense of it. Assemblage. Installation. Here, let me

untangle that. There, I unraveled the ball of yarn that guy's
been twining since 1967. Hiring a maid, a ready-made.

Half the time de-conundruming, the other half
upping the chaos, making the messes, messes of messes,

going, you call that a storm? I'll show you a storm, blasting
the viewer to Neptune's 900-mile-an-hour winds. Riddling the regular

with reindeer rivets. Oh, and better make sure it strikes a chord
any Hindu, hay-seed, or Yoruba can grok (grok that?).

But really it's just arranging, an arrangement, a bunch
of peonies, a couple irises, six long-stemmed roses. Not cut

and dried ones; real ones you put in water. Ungraspable's
good, too, as in stung like stinging nettle. As in this could be

a dream of eating ants, or this could be eating ants. But how,
you ask, did the Brillo pad scrub its way into a museum

my three year old could've built? Read above, where I mention
billboards, degree. What does art guide or guard? A whisper

of irony, a poke at documentary veracity, absurdity you may
or may not catch. I should hope it welcomes spies in the house

of serendipity, the calling into question of everything hanging
on every gallery's walls, but that's just my Jackson Pollock splatting.

And then there's wanting to crack the safe, break into that box
because tick-tock the game is locked. As in let me see, am I

seeing this right? It's a pill, isn't it? An insect eye? A sort of button
to push? A microcosm? A spaceship, no, yes, one of the 1,500

galaxies in Deep Field North? I knew it! I just knew it! A fertility goddess
walking her dog! Something that used to happen freely (freedom?)

that's recently been fenced. Something like feedlot confinement, I bet.
Or, no: I know! A subdivision, plans for the Fidalgo Bay Expansion,

complete with where the water will go. A trilobite? Or. She'd had
an identity and lost it. Her identity now orbiting like that 28,000-

km-per-hour glove dropped by a Gemini astronaut, the most dangerous
garment in history. Art is a dangerous garment. Art is a dress you don't

wear to work. Art's best kept with the cowboy poetry boots and the atheist-
patterned tights. Don't want to get art on your face, either. It might

make your neighbor edgy, especially if you ask him to share his thoughts
about the imagination. Discuss, instead, mowers, whether to go

with gas or electric. Ask to borrow his edger. Ask if it's time
your lawn had more edge. Or. She'd never been one for solving riddles,

but she liked a good joke. And fences make good neighbors.

HER PANEL

is a smooth-legged diction vixen
is go-go booted
Boolean

is a tribute to the demystified domestic
to the mystic
to the frisky

this many-gendered-splendor investigation
is a play date collaboration
is a get-me-a-glass-of-water praline

her panel with wainscoting
tongue and groove
her panel with structural insulation

her panel spitting drill bits
a chalk-lined congregation
her miter box panel effervescing

her caulking gun holy pink pagoda panel
poster girl decorative/Post cereal destructive
glitzy geisty grammared

her panel with increased octagonality
for our myriad beeswax
her hybridizing reclamation panel

for the rec room for the den
for a zig-zag ribbon of pedagogical glue
for the splintering syntax

her groovy speculative
her idiosyncratic spackling
her plumb subgenre

celebrating nine billion years
of cosmologic plot
honoring stats shen studs flarf

her panel a puffy pink hats-off to maraschino
her panel high-kickingly intertextual
her panel with flamboyant shims

her post-panelist theory panel
her observant subservient subversion panel
her panel of nail-biting blind-nailing veneer

her panel with flowing lava temptress
her proto-Crisco cage fight panel
her erudite exploratory pneumatic air gun panel

her adds-a-warm-glow contextualized leveler panel
her fashion-craving-framboise fuck you cathartic panel
her panel better than your panel

SANTIAGO SAYS

he isn't giving me laughing gas, he's giving me local;
he's got a needle but it's not the needle, not the local

that's calming me down; it's the loco, the totally loco,
as in the last time my mother came to town, she took

one look at my brown furniture, shipped it all to Goodwill.
Swabbing my gums with cherry mint goop while his mom's

letting loose, in his house, a piñata. It's like Mardi Gras threw up
in my den, Santiago's saying, my diseased mouth propped open

while he scrapes; but that's nothing. My dad? He worked, you know,
in commercial wiring. So, this one time he goes *touch that* and I'm like

is it hot? And he's all of course not, no, no, go ahead. So I touch it
and it knocks me out. Know what he says? *Don't trust nobody.*

But you know my brother had to get me back for all that shocking-
him-with-the-car-battery- every-morning stuff. He's an arsonist

investigator. Anyway, I'm like is that a Taser? Got me back all right.
Scars to prove it. I've never had a dentist scrape so hard, never knew

I had so much crud on my bones, so much periodontal hardship,
never knew I had, of all things, pockets, but one day my mom—

she works, you know, for Fish & Wildlife—comes home one day
to my dad in the backyard, dressing out a moose. In March. The only one

in the family with steady, upstanding employment, and her husband
in plain view with a poached animal. He's yelling *but he was stalking me!*

and she's after him with a lead pipe. And now Santiago's waving
his cleaning tool like a little weapon, and now he's shining me up,

shining the teeth I came into this world with, the ones I'll be buried
or burned with, the ones that know all my dirty little grinding

and clenching secrets. But then Santiago's back to his brother,
how he's a Casanova; after his first divorce he revamped his apartment—

juke box, pool table, full bar in the living room, buncha black lights.
If he meets a woman who'd put up with that, maybe he'll re-marry.

So he gets our aunts over there; next thing you know they're in the bedroom.
Man, he's saying, Aunt Suzie can really pole dance! And now it's the final rinse,

and spit's flying everywhere, saliva ejector ejected, and in this pastel office—
with these sober mini-blinds, this poor, puffy up-and-down chair—

and I'm choking on account of the little brother who believed for years
he was an orphan, left on the back porch, dressed like a little Eskimo.

Even took an interest in native cultures, cuz his big brother Santiago
Look! You're not one of us! How could you be? We're fifteen months apart!

On account of Santiago's you oughta be glad we got these needles,
cuz instead of laughing? You'd be leaving teeth marks on a bullet.

ODE TO IMAGINATION

and image, Vostok 1 hurling Yuri Gagarin
200 miles above us, what the optic nerve's

efforant fibers unstitch, then carry its post-
orbit parachuting news to the retina. News

the earth is blue, so we look and when we do
our brain's not calling up a replica from its cache

of Polaroids stuffed in an attic drawer,
but a brand new view of *vortex, tundra, crashed,*

of John Glenn's capsule, with John Glenn inside!
At the point of re-entry, his tin-can home sustaining

quadruple-digit temps. How are you imagining it?
I'm seeing half a dozen loafered, skinny-tied guys

cozied around a computer the size of the Gorge
in George, Glenn, squeezed in, bolted-up, triple-checking

Friendship's gauges. Fragile, fragile like an eggshell,
a cool, crisp morning in August. And Glenn,

not much good at *like* or *as*, with no *small steps*
or *giant leaps* up his space-suited sleeve *the sky*

in space is very black. This moment of twilight
is very beautiful. . . Okay, so we can't all be Keats,

and besides, could a scop have stood the stress of a strap
from the retropackage swinging around, fluttering

past the capsule window? Would you've preferred
the poet-astronaut spurting metaphors as the smoking

apparatus ignites? Glenn kept his white-knuckled wits,
and the rest is Apollo 11, the ghost drum ungoblined,

the silent victory trumpet triumphant, a halo go round
the moon. But back to image, the flash in the dark,

back to the viewer taking it in *Mama, wanna see,*
wanna see? Mama, you're not looking! Mama lifting off

in her Cosmodrome, to a place where image meets
interference, life by a thousand shadows, the interplay

between brain and eye working overtime
to lift us off this earth.

THE LITTLE OFFICE OF THE IMMACULATE CONCEPTION

REPORT FROM CONNECTICUT ON THE LETTER M, THE AB PATTERN, THE COUNTING BY 2S, 3S, AND 4S

It's the first week of kindergarten.
Draw a picture of the moon

his homework calendar states,
but tonight the moon

is nowhere to be found, buried
beneath clouds. Besides,

we're on the other side of the country,
having flown to a wedding

where nothing begins with M
except money and mojito,

mergers and martinis, a set
of M&M golf club gloves.

We are, however, making note
of all AB patterns, including

one chocolate chip, one cashew
(repeat, repeat), including

his little sister's mind-numbing repetitions:
ladeeladeeladeeladee, pluuuu. So we are, sorta,

doing homework, sorta making sense
of the patterns of triangles on the back

of our seats (light blue, blue, light blue, blue),
of the cat, dog, cat, dog ad for a bank

as we're waiting to board. But the planes
lining up for take-off are neither moon

nor discernible pattern. What do we do with those?
When we get home I promise to make him count

by 2s and 3s and even 4s, have him paste,
to a giant piece of paper,

cutouts of mittens and mice, of meercats and men,
but right now I'm helping him fasten his seatbelt

while holding my baby in my lap, right now I can't think
about patterns or numbers or even the moon, how certainly

it will outlast us.

THE NORM HAS A STANDARD DEVIATION
OF PLUS OR MINUS ELEVEN

but still they weigh us down, steady as sun—
never knee-jerk, more nictitating than nicotine-d,
never knocking glasses of vodka with jittery knees,

never scraping, while driving their cars, walls
of concrete. They don't even have a word
for losing, but if they did it would be smooth and wide,

and it would rhyme with win. When we offer them pity,
condolences, empathy's tilting head, they're not
befuddled or cross but usually unusually generous.

We, on the other hand, like tempest-battered,
un-battened teacups, are both the eye and the backside—
are also the deadly swath.

WHAT ARE YOU READING?

—question at a dinner party

Finches—their reluctance to visit her feeder. Dirt in a fuchsia-filled pot.
Venus and Jupiter, low in the western sky. Jupiter, closer than it's been in a while.

The kitchen towel's heretofore unnoticed ochre.
The marquee the marquee the marquee . . . .

Corn chip pretzel roasted pine nut barefoot Braille on a dining room rug.
Three-way billboard just before the slats slip into meaning.

Because I might need one, the 12 definitions of crown.
Because I might need it, the 5th definition of congress.

Spots on my Spanish teacher's skirt.
Leopard print skirt not once but twice in a row.

Date on a package of yeast. Umber of tracked-in leaves.
Feel of the dough feel of the dough . . . Tools. A mud-caked trowel.

Of the many shades of dying, of the many realms.
Crumbs on this quarter stick of butter. Crumbs of this bread . . .

GEOGRAPHY LESSON

I was thinking I should move to Goblin Valley
I was thinking in a place like Goblin Valley
they'd take me in complete with my
invisible pulse double-jointed fingers

pocky occipital nerve penchant for smolt-regurgitating terns
I didn't think I'd be welcome at the Crossing of the Fathers
even if it is just a bridge to another piece of land
especially not after telling my husband

all his belching left me feeling I'd spent the night in a dumpster it seems
downright oxymoronic a place called Thousand Lake Mountain
& yet I've seen corn stalks poking from why not call it
bedrock & yet I've heard my cousin in the Half Way

Baptist Church hit a note until that moment humanly impossible
these things happen like airplanes a few physics problems
holding them up when I go I'm taking the scenic route
Scenic Route say 12 the same way you'd say

what? 7:30? Fine *chuckchuckpurrrrrrr* my red Toyota pick-up
the ghosts of Uncles Benny William Peter Aunts Lottie Sophie
of course Helen who'd've packed a batch of her apricot-filled
cookies probably uses lard but o they're good

WHAT THE OLD WIVES TOLD ME

Nauseous? Must be a boy.
Wretching? Girl, girl, girl.

Carrying high? That's ambition—
your very own fetal valedictorian.

Carrying low? O woe: he won't
stop saying *nuclear pig* till he's 27.

The kicker? She's a cartographer,
sketching continents more remote

than Atlantis. Won't flip over?
He'll teach skydiving. Now it's time

to mix your urine with Drano
(good news/bad news: blue

could be either/both). Did you say
a circular motion? Fat and acne

all over? This is the body's way of saying
enough already with the turbulent

trampolining, the rampageous gymnastics.
Honey, why are you even asking?

Either one'll dig up your seedlings,
eat through to your tarnished

heart. Either won't stop saying
I want the cat pillow long after

you've given it back. Here's the baby
Heimlich maneuver, here's

a little mirror for the dash.
You'll get the hang of it—

the bouncing and the hushing
they always fall for, the baby

and the bathwater.

THE LITTLE OFFICE OF THE IMMACULATE CONCEPTION

   is almost always closed. More good news: no place
to kneel, no place to leave off applications,
though also no place for asking *how in the world?*

Hail, Queen Spermicide Dodger! Hail, Mistress
of the Quicker than Quickie! Hail, nothing close
to a virgin, of the messy-as-all-get-out birth!

Soiled diaper of the morning, shit enshrin'd!
O half-pint half drank, make speed to the help
of humankind. O my quiver, my queen of puppies,

mother of all goats and one purple unicorn. Mistress
of the aphid, who forsakest no one and despiseth no one
(except her brother, mostly when he swipes—except

her brother, when he swipes). Look upon me
with an eye of pity, o gherkin who'll soon be grown,
for I am the one who washes thine blueberry-stained bibs,

who droppeth to her knees to wipe up the milk
and the meat. Celebrate with devout affection
thy holy and immaculate conception, which by the way

is actually the story of bypassing a dousing
of Non-Oxynol 9. So, hereafter, by the grace
of Him whom thou, liveth and reigneth in perfect

purple and orange plaid skort. Hail, munchkin
most moist! Hail, seven furry caterpillars, the table
scribbled with brown and blue ink. Hail, new word: ant.

O perpetual snot! O paperclip in your mouth!
O gate you're stuck behind (with good reason)!
O lost marbles! O pure arc from changing table

to bathtub, fair rainbow of stench. Hail and dwell
in the highest, hail purity, which lasts about two seconds.
My lily among bits of plaster, dying parsley, keeling over

kale, spent tomatoes. Thanks to you, dear bombardier,
I'm the mother of mercy. Thanks to you I give hope
to the guilty. You with your three pink blankets,

you with your avocado smears, you drooling olives.
Me with my need to straighten, my need for quiet,
right here in this little office, this little

immaculate office, where a healthy glob
of pharmaceutical this-and-that couldn't stop you.
O rage! O sperm! O last of my healthy eggs!

Here where we cooked you up
like a cherry-almond tart—cinnamon, flour, butter
(1 1/4 cold unsalted sticks). Coarse crumbs worked

to a ball. Let us pray, holy girl, though not
in martyrdom's palm; let us pray, enthralled.

POEM AFTER VALLEJO

This ruby-red rope that rasps, that wraps me up, arrests
my total unraveling. I was not raped. I was not ripped
from childhood. I was given time, acres of acorn squash time,

to ripen before I was snipped from the vine.
And I am not a mother of twelve, not the village idiot
of a Southern Italian town, so why am I mourning? (my bones

not strangers, not strangers at all). Because desire,
desire like the tigers yanked from our local zoo, desire's
been exiled to Kansas—a field of winter wheat, a farm house

far from other farms, a farm wife who kills her meat,
who also has her hoeing, her milking. *This ruby-red rope that rasps,*
more than a door that doesn't close, more than the green leaves no longer

applauding. My former life's been seized and I'm seething,
unsootheable, unsoundlessly sleeping. This life's better than the one
before but still I'm dangling *from this endless rope like a spiral descending. . .*

EMERGENCY COMFORT KIT

Inside, we should place a blanket, one that folds to the size
of a toy kazoo. A light stick, the kind kids love

to swirl at the darkening sky. He needed six hand wipes,
a pack of Kleenex, his name on a 3 x 5 card.

A small cozy toy made sense; we knew which ones
we couldn't take away, but the one he would need that day—

which? The 30-gallon trash bag: a poncho of course.
A family photo—*for comfort*—but also identification.

We were to tell ourselves these were ordinary measures,
thoughts to store away in the bottom-most drawer,

on the farthest, most unreachable shelf. That the likelihood
of needing the raisins was slim, that even when a blizzard

disabled all our county's buses, most of the children
slept that night in their beds. This was routine,

and the cans of apple juice would never be punctured,
and the letter, like the looks on our faces,

would never be read.

WHERE'S OUR DIGNITY?

She's hanging out in malls. She's up there swinging
with the climate controls, with the dusty, greasy
lingering-from-the-'60s *give me a hotdog and a Pepsi* exhaust.
Swooning, pre-baguette, pre-lime-infused Evian.
She's gotten wind of vents that gulp down noise,
but not her cracking gum. Invisibly lurks
through grandiose bathrooms, innocent
as freesia, as faucets sensing the heat
of hands. Promising connectivity gateways,
she's bought a laptop but hasn't logged on.
Released like jello from an aluminum mold,
she reminds us of the 54 billion galaxies,
then retreats to the slot in our broken-
since-1999 VCR. In the unlikely event
of a water landing, she's our stalwart
flotation device. When we lean in ("Eternity,
do you like it?"), when we peel yet another
$100 bill from our money clip (not
for the homeless, AIDS, Cystic Fibrosis,
The American Red Cross), she shakes
a bony finger: "Stretch Lycra, stretch limo—
it's all the same in the end."

POOR BANISHED CHILDREN OF EVE

I WANTED TO BE HIP

but with a kid strapped into the stroller
my size 38EE breasts my husband

accidentally *hi there mammary glands*
but with not knowing which belt

black with silver studs or multi-colored sash
which sandals wedge or flip-flop

then which flip-flop beaded or bangled
instead I got escorted to the elevator for the un-hip

child on each hip for the totally un-tuned-in
though all of us wanted to emanate

snake skin pumps a sparkly amber shawl
so we might gesticulate with flair

wanted let's face it the whole world to wobble
when we watusied into a room

chins jutting never tucked under
like a sleeping gull more like mama killdeer

feigning a broken wing
Remember the first hip huggers?

I thought it was 1968
but my US Navy dad dug in his closet

to 1944 found the sailor suit
complete with low-rise bell bottoms almost

killed him he couldn't button up

AFTER READING THERE MIGHT BE
AN INFINITE NUMBER OF DIMENSIONS

I'm thinking today of how we hold it together,
arrive on time with the bottle of Zinfandel, a six-pack

of Scuttlebutt beer, how we cover our wrinkles
with Visible Lift, shove the mashed winter squash

into the baby's mouth, how we hold it all together
despite clogged rain gutters, cracked

transmissions, a new explanation for gravity's
half-hearted hold. I'm wondering how we do it,

comb the tangles from our hair, trim the unwieldy
camellia, speak to packed crowds about weight loss

or fractals. I'm wondering how we don't
fall to our knees, knowing a hardened pea,

lodged in the throat, can kill, knowing
liquids are banned on all commercial flights.

Leaves fall. The baby sucks her middle fingers.
Meanwhile, the refrigerator acquires

an unexplainable leak. Meanwhile, we call
the plumber, open wide for the dental hygienist,

check each month, with tentative circlings,
our aging breasts. Somehow, each morning,

the coffee gets made. Somehow, each evening,
the crossing guard lifts her fluorescent orange flag,

and a child and her father cross the glistening street.

POOR BANISHED CHILDREN OF EVE

I believe in the dish in the sink
not bickering about the dish in the sink
though I believe the creator

of the mess in the living room
cleans up the mess in the living room
sucks up cracker pizza potpie peanut popcorn

and I believe in the earth which also ends up on the rug
which must also be vacuumed up as I acknowledge
our blessings running water not teeming with toxins

and even though this might sound like nagging
especially in the face of dying and of burial
and of purgatory and of hell especially when

I could be instead of asking could you please
wipe up the olive juice that little pile of parsley
wailing and moaning at your wake

or maybe just sitting there stunned where beside me
sitteth the six year old and the 19 month old who most definitely
wouldn't get the dying concept though maybe the son

from thence being the owner of two dozen dead ladybugs
And I believe in the holy in the hole in the toe
of his feet-in pajamas *Mama look how much I grew*

in just one night! His reminder I own a sewing kit
and also all the holy saints (especially the martyrs)
the resurrection of peace-sign pasta three nights running

and the father of course thy will be done
though in fact a whole lot doesn't get done
like fixing the cracked windows re-upping prescriptions

or dusting let's not forget dusting hallowed be the trip
to Safeway for lettuce yogurt our daily beer
and lead us away from bitching about picking up

the hallowed son from the bus-stop
lead us away from resenting the filing
the trips to the curb to the bank

lead us away from martyrdom
(though did we mention we love the saints)
lead us away from the temptation to chuck it all flee

to Thetis Island and glory be to dishwashing liquid
and the sponge glory to the microwave and Mr. Coffee
for the world and all its Huggies all its wet wipes

glory be and have mercy and save us from the pot
of boiling water from the fires otherwise known
as letting the smoke-alarm battery go dead

to thee do we cry poor banished children of Eve
poor ants at the mercy of unforeseen disaster
poor praying mantises stuck in our plastic cages

poor and thankless a valley of tears
though actually a giant crevasse
grant us eternal grant us merciful
o clement o loving o sweet

THAT SPRING A ROOM APPEARED

in their house, a room they hadn't
been in, a room they didn't know

they had. *Maybe it's a tent—easy to disassemble*, poles
clearly marked, stakes pulling up with only the slightest

tug, though this addition—in it was a curtain rod
like a drum majorette's abandoned baton. In it

was a cricket, incessant chirper (and what
was it chirping? *fuck fuck fuck fuck. . .*).

A room they didn't know existed,
and in that room a couple could make love,

but when they did they closed their eyes
like wincing. And in that room *bed*

meant shrinking away like the tentacles
of an anemone. Outside, seeds were sown—

mesclun and spinach, outside
raking leaves revealed perennials—

hyacinth, iris, bleeding heart—
but in that room the teapot broke,

the porch light popped, the couch contracted
a cough. In that room the Dick Van Dyke Show

without the laugh track, and instead of longing
for sprinklers, for the light that stretches past ten o'clock,

they fell into loving the cold (*damn birds, would you please shut up*).
And in that room the toast they found in the toaster

at lunch, the chimeless chimes, the dusty, dying ficus,
the coffee they'd reheated hours ago. And then

the snow that fell on the mossy roof, snow that caked
to the bottom of their skis like a bad case of clown feet—

snow they tried to shake off, bang off, wax off. Or one
ski slick, one stuck; one revving to go, the other no way in hell.

They had things to say, but the room made them tired,
so they slept, so they tried to sleep, tried to decide:

should they head down (icy, steep), or should they park it
right here. Should they just park it—cut

the engine, shovel down to the dirt, back 'er up?
Wanting the room to go away, wanting anything

but the coffee cold, the microwave's digital readout:
End. . . End. . .End. . .

YOU'RE LIKE THE MEAN MAN

You're like the mean man with the newspaper; he's like my wife. You're not turning the page, the way my wife won't turn toward me in bed. You're the mean man with the glazed donut of an idea; he's a scientist, like my wife with her parallel glaze, my wife in the bed with her Bunsen burner, her Kama Sutra, her commas, her *wanna don't wanna*. He's like my wife, which means you're a mean newspaper man, a plan, a man with news, today's news, which is her three trillion dollar deficit in the meaning and feeling department, in understanding the meaning of what is meant. He's mean, you're mean, we're all mean wives with sharp sticks in our hair, mean Hubble spacecraft take-off mouths. When she comes to terms with the term *output reduction*, every man knows she means less.

LOVE

with apologies to Julie Sheehan

I hate your kneecaps floating free
in their salty baths. I hate your knees,

both of them, and I hate your eyelashes,
especially the ones that fall out, the ones

you're supposed to wish on; I wish you
bad wishes. I hate every hair

on your hairy face, hate you as much
as I hate being put on hold,

thank you for your patience
when I have none, when patience

is as far away as my first grade teacher's
if you have nothing nice to say. . .

Your mushroom risotto: hate it.
The salmon you're defrosting: hate.

My vowels hate you.
My adverbs hate you. The backyard

hates you—the backyard with all its abandoned
dump trucks, with the giant hole our son dug

all summer while soaker hoses soaked. That hole
and all holes, including the hole in the ozone,

which of course keeps growing bigger.
Spaghetti wrapping around a fork.

Mashed spinach and carrots caught
in the rungs of a high chair, stuck

to the floor like dried green paint: hate,
hate, hate. Each furry rabbit a little furry ball

of hate. Each blackberry a messy drupe of drippy hate.
At the China Palace the plates piled high with Mu Shu

Hate, the plates now a busboy's burden of hate,
the only sound the dumpster's clanging *hate hate hate*.

HATE

is maybe too strong a word maybe what you want is reasoned thought
though really this has little to do with you is maybe the one time a person's
granted immunity from critical anything enough with the A

to B and more loads more of the 2 plus 2 equals 3,964
maybe what I want for you is pain though at this
even the coming-up-with-revenge-plans part

I stink not even when my roommate kicked me out for one measly story
only roughly based on a single part of her not-really-very-interesting-
or-intriguing life could I and it wasn't even my idea

but my boyfriend's even imagine sending her in the US mail a giant rotten trout
which does prove one thing I for instance was taught not to not even
when it strummed my guts like those instruments

made from (what else?) guts even when it coursed and suctioned
like a pulsing benthic octopus who watching for half a year
over her rice-sized eggs eats nothing

who just before dying gently blows her hatchlings from the den
of course toward you who at best won't read the sign who at worst
will describe with of course one of them in your mouth their sumptuous flesh

which is not to say I don't eat eggs cod pork screaming Romaine
which is not to say rationality wins but rather that all it means
is *extreme animosity* deriving from of all things Latin
for *courage* and *bold* words like *spirit* like *soul*

CRICKETS, GOD, PHAN KU, PICKLES, SYNERGY, A WAYSIDE CHURCH, ANAXAGORAS, ANAXIMANDER, MORE CRICKETS, THE COSMOS

And in her house, crickets—beneath the refrigerator, crouched
behind the chopping block, nibbling last week's parsley. She feared

the chirping would stop, that come one evening she'd waken to silence,
but November and still their scraper-and-wing-slapping stridulation,

as if she's in some deepest Oregon, canned-pear-and-okra-crammed,
woodstove-warmed, off the grid, chickens-pecking-the-floor of-a lean-to,

when in truth buses *szzzzzzz* or squeaky-wheel by, when in truth
their freezer's crammed with fish sticks and fries. Her brother once told her,

God is waiting for you. He loves you; he wants you to accept his love.
But the only time she summons Him, catches a glimpse of his glimmer,

is when she dips into *there are roughly 100 billion galaxies, each containing*
100 billion stars. It's enough to leave her lurching for a banister

or a deity, though really not much different, in terms of lurching,
than learning that the Chinese, back in the day, believed

Phan Ku created humans when they fell as lice from his hair. And then
it's time for lunch, and she'll have the halibut sandwich, no tartar sauce;

pickles on the side. But no, too expensive, so home to crackers and Swiss.
But then again when a friend's friends are all dying, and this is his life now,

this and his gray bangs, this and his needing to ask the bartender to repeat
the names of the beers on tap three times. Because he's laughing, telling her

he can't believe he just said *synergy*, and she's telling him she's okay with it.
Or when she's on a plane and the captain gets on: *did you hear that pop*

a little ways back? That was one of our engines, so we shut 'er down. Pause. Luckily,
we've got another one, and it's working just fine (she, of course, please God, not

all over the suburbs of south Atlanta; please, because her children don't know
Bernoulli's principle isn't always enough). Or, she summons the Almighty

as a porcupine waddles toward her through the cattails, or down 5th Avenue,
looking up at a giant wrecking ball. But mostly the little wayside church

is boarded up; the plexiglass window has a sign, and the sign says *Sorry, Closed.*
Mostly because her father, when she told him there was a Magnolia Warbler

in the oak, said *yes, all those little canary birds,* she lives without Him despite
the apparent extinction, during the Cambrian, of all but a few of the brachiopods,

despite what Anaxagoras referred to as *the dense . . . the dark, the what-is*
cannot not be. Instead she has Anaximander's belief the moon and stars

are holes in a fire-drenched sky. Instead she has the crickets,
the crickets and the cosmos—its root in *to order, to organize.*

MORE WAVES MAY FOLLOW

THIS PARENTING THING

which I love which I hate
the love part easy not torture at all

like his asking *spell furniture* while we wait
outside the Rogue River Fly Shop

like checking to see if the faeries came
his digging with a blue shovel while I weed

the broccoli the kale and even asking
over and over for a gummy worm

which I will not give him he's already
had three and that's just the beginning

the first few words of the brook
that flashes and foams that keeps on

with its garter-snake awe with its ant fascination
all of it not yet drooped not yet fallen in a heap

till all that's left is a rose hip
a hip you could dry and make a tea with

but will you? But that's the least of it
barfing croup a temperature of 105

the day he mistook motor oil for bubble bath
the day he ate the insect repellant *just be lucky*

they're healthy how dare you hate his sneakiness
his thrown-out crusts just be lucky you don't live

in Nigeria where polio's making a comeback
just be glad you don't live nearly anywhere else

but what about my one-year old her three or four
or sometimes fifteen nighttime feedings

can I hate what sleeplessness does to a brain
like I'm caught in amber whenever

multi-cellular beings formed
dragging along reaching for sugar caffeine

like some ammonite some primitive mollusk
a little closer I'll admit to all that lives

but not quite sane when she starts to choke
on a piece of grocery list the firemen storming

where is she? to de-lodge the marble or dime
to turn her upside down and whack her

till the bead or pebble slips out
though by the time they arrive

I've pulled out the guilty party and she's cooing
Love it? Love it? Yep yep especially

the notes that come from school
Riley helped a sad friend today

or looking up to see in place of her face
a lime green plastic plate anticipating

my *peek-a-boo!* though could live without
the half-way through yoga right when we're about

to start on shoulder stands *I think she wants
her mama* though bet you'd find it hard to believe

feeding her mashed peas and rice I'm already
longing for the silver and turquoise spoon

for what falls to her sleeve but then she's screaming
and I'm screaming over her screaming

carrying on the conversation hating
what she takes longing for evening's relief

though longing too for morning though dreading the bib
and the apple sauce wriggling her into pink plush jeans

though not wanting her anywhere close
to asking for keys and meanwhile my son

can't stop asking where is it who has it
and all about the kid who owns it now

forever and ever until he discovers there's one with spots
and that one will do which lasts about fifteen minutes

my whole life snatched away for procurement forms
for reading him *Goodnight Moon* and *Click, Clack, Moo*

for lifting her up to the doctor's scale
watching the numbers line up

SHE HAD SOME TANTRUMS

with apologies to Joy Harjo

She had some tantrums.

She had tantrums who were one order of Kung Pao chicken and four forks.
She had tantrums who were Sky Cab and a gate change.
She had tantrums whose drill bits broke through diamonds.

She had some tantrums.

She had tantrums who were petri dishes filled with slime mold.
She had tantrums who caught a glimpse of a Skittle.
She had tantrums who would not sign a peace treaty.

She had some tantrums.

She had tantrums who were the ax murderer of Smuttynose Island.
She had tantrums who demanded pink icing and rainbow sprinkles.
She had tantrums requiring a Warning Sequence.

She had some tantrums.

She had tantrums who unlike the lemurs of Madagascar were not gravely endangered.
She had tantrums who barked and boomed, the vocal pouch swelling like a balloon.
She had tantrums who were vomit on a Lilli Pulitzer dress.

She had some tantrums.

She had tantrums who said *fanny*.
She had tantrums who never saw the green anole.
She had tantrums who smashed through Grenada, The Windward Islands
and Quintana Roo.

She had some tantrums.
She had tantrums with a hairdo like Einstein.
She had tantrums like a flock of turkey vultures on a road-kill squirrel.
She had tantrums with electroplated fists.

She had Cimarron tantrums.

She had tantrums with bullwhips and vapor cones.
She had tantrums where the goal is to put five consecutive shots
into a single hole no larger than the diameter of the bullet.
She had tantrums emitting the sulfurous fumes of Vulcano.

She had some tantrums.
She had videotaped tantrums and WebCam tantrums.
She had pristine tantrums and grimy tantrums.
She had kickboxing tantrums and Pilates tantrums.

Let me tell you, she tantrumed.

She had tantrums that zinged like a Pflueger Summit Fly Reel.
She had tantrums that punctured ear lobes, tongues, noses.
She had tantrums that made you want to tie a t-shirt around your ankles and walk
through tall grasses, hoping to squeeze out a little water.

She wrote the book on tantrums.

She had tantrums that ignited 180,000 acres.
She had tantrums needing 950,000 gallons of retardant.
She had tantrums calling in, from 24 states, 2,400 firefighters.

She had some mother fucking tantrums.

She had tantrums that made you want to forget to have your appliances equipped
with carbon monoxide detectors.
She had tantrums that made you want to laugh your ass off.

These were the same tantrums.

THIS IS NOT A LULLABY

We were having the usual fight, not the good fight,
the one demanding health care, clean water for all,

not the one insisting gay marriage, the right to choose,
but the one about sunburned shoulders, who forgot

to pack the sunscreen, the one about the single avocado
when we needed four. And then the trail headed off

into downward, into me alone, me and our news-to-me
Unwanted, where I could no longer tell if the whooshing

was the wind or a raging creek, where the lodgepole pines
were monsters. In this way I knew if I left the trail, stepped into

brushy ravine, nothing in my pack could save us, though I knew
through it all she'd be chattering about the ravens, their hypothetical

nest, how she needed to fly to it, help with the feeding, all the while
the lessening light, the becoming-mum forest, except for

If I was big and had a blog I'd fill it with lupine and paintbrush,
the quarter moon like an enormous fingernail on an enormous

wagging finger (*Why are we whispering, mama? Do you not want
to wake up the moon?*). No matches, no lighter, no blanket. Just the cold air—

you, me, and *the moon has no eyes so it can't be waked up,* my toadflax,
my stubborn thistle who wants not only to catch the fish but to remind it

how to breathe again in water, this girl bushwhacking with Medea:
two birds—the raspy warbling vireo and the trilling junco—one stone,

these first few steps where the snowbush doesn't give a damn,
though I could serve her dirt cakes, lies I'm already telling, lies that begin

lightning can't strike you if you're under a tree, telling her, when she asks,
dada and brother are just ahead, building a fire, opening cans of mushroom soup;

don't worry—I have the secret code; I know the language of stars. One minute
we were minutes away from the green-roofed houses, the path

to the road, the next I was leading my Salsify, my Three Blind
Mice songster, into nothing on a map.

MORE WAVES MAY FOLLOW

I told her *your hair has lovely waves*
so she waved like the white-gloved

Miss Merry Christmas on the Christmas float.
He said *my egg beater runned out of gas* because

it was his mower, the same one his father used
to keep the house from burning down. We do not

anticipate this, but if tables and chairs
begin to fall over, do not expect

another warning. When he heard me say
prosciutto he thought *pro-shoot-o*, so the tongs

a new kind of power, a weapon all his own.
Begin to fall over our only warning; there was no other.

I wish I could die he'd said so now he had his chance
(now I was surely listening). And I'd said

nothing negative (we were talking
about subtraction, how you can't take

four away from two), but this has nothing to do
with positive. They were expecting me

to save them, and that was a little jarring,
especially when I looked up Third Street, knew

it was floating with bodies. Do not pack
your belongings; don't recount your longings.

Every wrong thing you did had a reason.
She's running from me, won't let me

comb her hair; he wants to lie down
in the road, let the rushing run him over.

We are the waves. We are the numbers.
We are *no one's watching over us*

and *this is just what happens.*
We are the sinking, yet all the while

*we can go to another world—all we need to do
is doggy paddle*—our insurance, her hair ties,

his haiku with the springing deer—
all in a churn, our stay at the hotel

over, our only warning the falling.

POEM ENDING WITH THE INFAMOUS WORDS OF A BROTHER-IN-LAW

March 2002

A rockfish. A whole one, fried:
tail fin, pelvis, pectoral—

all of it caught mid-swish.
The couple sharing it grandly—

licking their fingers, exuding
a greasy glow; its mouth hanging open

I could say like it wanted to speak,
but really more simple—its final moments

a grease-choked hell. I asked
my father-in-law to turn around, to have

another look, but he was right—
it would be rude to gawk

at the cooked-at-high-heat-
with-splatters-and-hisses.

I was sure we wouldn't dare,
that no one would have the nerve,

but then *why not?* So there it was:
our own tempura-battered flecks,

our own white eyes where clarity
for years had pooled,

its sides now sprigged
with cilantro and basil, its preference

for continental shelves, for a home
in the Bering Sea, now rolled

in a pancake, dabbed
with a little hoisin.

The conversation tangy too
and crisp, as we spat out

the bones of the inner ear
drifted in the current

(a special gland for buoyancy
and venomous spines

we'd overlooked).
No one dies in wars anymore.

They hit their targets.
Who said anything about death?

9/11 ON 9/11/09

And just like that—eight years. Eight years, and Mama,
I know a pattern: red, beige, black, white, red, beige, black, white.

Saying *and turquoise—there has to be turquoise.* And indeed
there was a blinding blue, and *sparkly silver.* Asking

can we have this every day? while the voice on the radio
the very last thing I said to him was 'I love you;' the very last thing

he heard me say: I love you (his son a fireman, heading
for the sparkly silver, heading for red, beige, black, white).

My daughter was nowhere, and now she's four,
and it's a Friday like those no-planes days, those no-

sound-but-the-squeaking-swings days, days you could watch them
(the parents), hands shielding their eyes, squinting at the no-jet-trails

sky. She said *red.* I said yes, but I did not say blood. She said *beige,*
and I did not say, and brown skin too. She said *black,* and I thought

charred. She said *white,* but I did not say bone. Eight years
is a long time. Eight years is not a long time. The kids who saw it

on TV are nearly grown, asking to have their hair cropped close,
trailed by recruiters at the mall. The sky? It was unconscionably blue.

The billowy blue of a burka. Blue, as in red, white, and blue.
In some ways it was spacious; in some ways it was not.

She woke up saying *Mama, I know a pattern.*

TEN DAYS IN ARKANSAS

and on the final one she takes a walk
to the graveyard, past a row of loblolly pines,
resin sticking to her arms, resin like the names

of those beneath her—William Moon, Leroy Bliss.
She thought she'd find—under these loblollies,
under these silver maples—the long-married,

which of course she does—John and Ellen Gibson,
who held on close to a hundred years; Lucille
and Floyd Pruitt; Wendell Weed waiting

for his Margaret, but where she also finds,
in the Garden of Prayer, Laura Beanie Lehman,
who made it only to 30, whose husband Cecil

must be the one leaving the plastic roses,
and BJ Nicklas who didn't get past 25,
his father beside him; and as she's nearing

the exit gate, relieved to escape the faded
wreaths, the searing heat, she runs right into
Angelo Karimu, beneath his name a single

date, beside it a dirty white-winged bear,
not unlike the one her son won't
let go of, not for the life of him.

WOMEN ARE NOT ALONE AND THAT

's a good thing; we're not alone in the morning—
the whizzing and whisking, juice falling into glasses.

Women are not alone when the clock strikes eight
because that's when a small boy climbs the metal stairs

and waves, the mother waving back, but also to the mom whose
son just missed the bus. And women are not alone at lunch,

the clock now a mourning dove, the phone a rooster that overslept
I'm sorry I forgot your birthday, your anniversary, your grief,

which was also her birthday, our forgetting, our loss.
Women are never alone and that means the cherry tomatoes

are the friends we planted ourselves, not quite sure they'd visit
but they did. Ebullient, downright cheery as they split open, split

apart, stinging our tongues which are hungry for the past, for hearing,
over *pasta vongole*, over matsutake sukiyaki, what happened

before we were born; to piece it all together like a crown
of thorns; meanwhile, it's time to draw the baths.

HOW TO SEW

You need a mouthful of pins.
You need a Simplicity pattern,

the onion-skin sheets explaining—
with dotted lines, with numbers
and arrows—palazzo pants, a hooded dress.

The best part is the storeowner,
her rhinestone pince-nez glasses,

how she flips and flips your chosen bolt,
lavender fabric spilling out
like a colossal ribbon candy.

The best part is the sound of scissors
slicing through a poly-cotton blend.

You will need to learn
about edges, about gathers.

Meanwhile, the whole contraption
disguised to look like a table. Meanwhile,

lifting the lid, reaching in
for the smooth black cat, needle

for a mouth. Meanwhile, threading
the bobbin; the squeaking

of the foot pedal. You will discover
there is satisfaction in edgestitching.
Edgestitching and stitch ripping.

You will wear the flawed apron,
but only you will know the flaw.

You will learn to tie off knots.

THEY KNOW ALL ABOUT US ON ANDROMEDA

and why shouldn't they? We're flashy after all,
flashy and feisty with our pink quartz, our pyrite,

our bioluminescence, our radioactive. They're talking
about us in Ambartsumian's Knot, mostly because they covet

the nifty and myriad ways we unravel. Those who hail
from Seyfert's Sextet rave about our moon, the best companion

this side of the Tuft in the Tail of the Dog, cuz how many
celestial bodies rhyme with June and swoon? Zwicky's Triplet-ians

admire our syllabic glyphs in the eery Mayan light, and let me tell you:
they're triply wowed. In Fourcade-Feguaro they're green with our glibness,

our profusion of CO_2. And way out there in the Tadpole? They're thrashing
with the news of spontaneous generation, IM-ing our cloud-eating shark: LMIRL.

IT'S ALL GRAVY

BECAUSE I KNEW

you'd love my informational mobile made of
cold-snap-thwarting cotechini, because I knew

that rather than interview a bolas spider, you'd
dial me up on the last pay phone, the one out back

of Tacoma Screw. Because I knew it was *me-n-you*
like a cashmere-wool blend sock and the pair of leopard-

print panties it's electrically sticking to, I was wishing
for no red lights because you're Fantasia Fun Park,

the Red Dragon Casino, Rock and Roll's Greatest Hits.
Because you remind me harlequin bugs are doing it

in the delicata starts. I thought I'd hum you a little *oh
say can you see*, and you'd know this wasn't drunk driving,

more like drunk diving, drunk thriving. And you'd see too
that the arrows on the Exit-Only signs are heading straight

for our Earth's own heart, that cupid's arrows are everywhere,
desire the one thing uniting us all—leaf hopper, flamboyant

flower beetle, roly poly bug, and also whoever painted *Hot
Sexy Baristas!* on the take-out window of Sweet Shots.

Though we tell ourselves our top speed's a little faster
than a kangaroo, a little slower than an elephant,

how do we really know, with our blinkers on,
untethered, whisking through endless space? On our way

to toll booths, picket lines, to cutting boards on which
we'll chop hundreds of onions, crying, wiping our eyes,

crying as we arrive in cookie cutter neighborhoods with our rags
and our vacuums, speeding along at 70,000 miles per hour,

even as the engine's cooling in our last-chance parking lot.
Because I knew you'd understand this—you, me, our sibling

earthlings, our sibling citizens of this swirly world,
which only grows bluer the farther away from it we get.

YOUR LAUNDRY ON THE LINE LIKE A GIANT, BREATHING BEAST

Your laundry on the line like a giant, breathing beast,
like the billowing sheets above the alleys in Trastevere,

where mothers yell after their children *Vieni qua! Vieni qua!*
while underwear sways like language itself. Rippling and tossing,

the tie-dyed tank in a snit because you've hung it beside
the light-blue flowered PJs; the white briefs mingling

with the black briefs (*do you think we're as good
as the purple-striped?*). Though you can't begin

to explain the sorrow of pulleys, the care a woman takes
to add a little bluing to the twirl of skivvies and socks,

to load a long and squeaky rope with Wranglers and BVDs,
you'll be the first to say this is not that clothesline,

though there is sorrow, a touch of sorrow, in the faces
of certain t-shirts, in the hummingbird that ticks and buzzes

at the Bermudas, expecting nectar from a fabric hibiscus.
You can't exactly say you like your chores, but there is,

you'll admit, a certain reward in the rinsing and wringing,
in filling a wicker basket with the sweet clover and Solomon plume

of satisfaction, the behemoth of things needing doing
laid down, for a time, to rest.

THANKFUL QUITE THANKFUL

for the thin clear soup
the old man who shuffles along
as if he might be carrying
in that steamy bowl
all our children's futures

for this and for the chicken
the blood that swirled
the cook who peeled the forty cloves

don't tell me you've been oversleeping
all your subscriptions expired
and no access to cable

actually I bet you couldn't balance a checkbook
I mean if humanity were a Fortune 500
we'd've fired you a couple millennia ago

none of us ever did like the prima donnas
who show up for weddings
but where are they when you need
for instance help with moving?

spider webs and the crab nebulae aside
what sort of comfort are cooing doves
the half-honk half-squeak of herons?

Thankful quite thankful
for the suctioned legs of an octopus
that color like a bruise
for Superglue and the woman
who served up (grumpily
with a few swift thwacks)
the best pizza in all Sicily

praise the lawn
boisterous with beetles
praise the wide windows
out of which we see

the Hing Loon restaurant
though mostly this thin clear soup
this bowl so carefully

WAY OVER THERE

Everyone gets their phonics homework done on time
everyone makes a snow globe
and the little cardinal stuck

to the bottom of a baby food jar
never comes unglued
mommy in fact

never comes unglued and the daddy
(part Mr. Brady part Clark Kent
just a smidgen

of Arnold Schwarzenegger thrown in)
can't wait to come home and empty
the trash make a dent

in the mountain of dirty pots & pans
& the kids never lose their breath
turn blue while the medics

clamor up the walk with the oxygen tank
never need to be tested for thirteen
allergies including Cat Epithelium

the son happy with his wooden dinosaurs
never crying *'puter mama 'puter!*
the daughter never waking

with a fever—barf all over her puppy-patterned dress
& after the kids go to bed the mommy (half-
Demi Moore half-Angelina Jolie) dons
an apron with nothing underneath
nothing except a Miracle Bra
a red lacy thong

no burnt-out light bulbs no crumbs in the sheets
way over there not even on the shortest day
all the money and time and love they need

REGRETS ONLY, PLEASE

I like to travel, might even call myself an extrovert, don't mind
striped socks or a bulbous nose, so why didn't I apply

to Clown College? I should've listened more
to that wise old owl who, the more he listens,

the less he talks, the less he talks the more he hears,
should've engaged more often, and with more vigor,

my bundas, which are the core muscles, the ones
holding it all together; occasionally, to show how much

I love him, should've asked for The Tail of the Ostrich,
however tough on the spine and neck. I didn't pay attention

to my mother, or more so, my grandmother, especially
when she spoke of General Cigar—the exact number,

on a given day, she'd rolled. When she died
& I looked up at the first sunset since August 27, 1912

without her on this earth, I kept getting distracted
by the loudspeaker, announcements for a flight

to Kalispell. I should've learned from my father
what makes a polymer twist. From my sister the art

of rewiring a lamp, something, however small,
about trowels. From my brothers how to carry a tune

while sober. I should've been one of those people
who assembles rockets, maneuvers with ease

the tightest cave, unravels DNA. When I saw,
the week *e. coli* poisoned all that hamburger,

a Jack-in-the-Box sign announcing *Hiring*
for Graveyard, where was my camera? I always stop

at wayside chapels, but never get out of my car. And o
those nimbly swinging gorillas, the outrageous clatter of toucans.

NO REFUNDS, NO EXCHANGES

Across the yard, despite a fierce unrest,
I can't help noticing the smudged chin

of an English sparrow, ululations
of cedar waxwings, robins slick

in the sloppy rain. If there were footprints,
they would be cloven. If this were an orchard,

the apples would glow like the polished floors
of my twenties and thirties. Not many hearts

have lifted like swallows to the cliffs
above Pomme de Terre Lake, not many

have lived much closer than five doors down
from God. And yet I'm no girdle

on this galaxy's expanding waistline,
and yet I've no sacred cows worth swimming

to the South China Sea and back for.
Each morning the silent coyotes

disappear behind my window's dusty slats
just as an all-night cat in heat slips a paw

through her little cat door. My morning coffee
tastes of the earth, a cell or two of every creature

who's padded or paddled, crept or crawled,
slithered or swam, who's foisted a pincer

on an unsuspecting worm. Earwig. Juggler.
Jaguar. Saint. Bombardier riding shotgun

on a leaf held high by an ant.

SHALL I COMPARE THEE TO A SPRING DAY AT THE NAPLES ZOO?

I'm not sure thou art more temperate, but thou surely art
less feline, less toothsome, less crawling with kids in strollers.
I doubt any rough winds will be shaking anything till at least
late June, but already the hot eye of heaven is bearing down
(if we don't glob on the Water Babies soon, we'll be as red
as these scarlet macaws). But you really art this spring day,
especially these anoles our kids can't stop stalking. Art,
for sure, unlike our daughter shouting *The End! Done!*
before our boat ride even begins, a little eternal, in the way
calmly breezy and 80 degrees is not. Death's not going to boast
you wander in his shade—oh, no—cuz we've got this awning
to stand under while we wait for our trip to Monkey Island.
Cuz I've remembered to pack, along with the sunscreen,
animal crackers and wet wipes, my notebook and pen.

IN THE SLAUNCHWISE WORLD

In this one she grades Kenny's essay, changes the oil, purchases snacks for ride home.
In this one she grasps the meaning of manifold.
In this one she has the answer regarding infinity.

Bio goes thus:

Raised by baffled fingers, her days involve pencil end chewing and other miracles. Sweeping, she makes her home in candy cigarettes.

or

While bear claws sweat in cellophane, she senses the toilet is overflowing. She lives and works in a moss-covered '68 Mustang.

or

A dust-is-the-only-secret fan, she fashions spheres from paper napkins; with these she bowls.

In this one she understands Persephone's bargain with Hades.
In this one she never breaks the spaghetti, always sends a thank you.
In this one there's a phenol Barbie doll.
In this one the rubric is a redbrick.
In this one the drum always drains.
In this one she remains fragile.

EASTER VISIT

Her poofy pink dress had a hole in it long before Jesus staged
His annual comeback, her Mary Jane's brown with Ozark mud

before there was even a rumor of rising. The plastic egg grandma would find
on her lawn next week hadn't yet been filled with a rubbery squid.

Her daughter/their mother had fallen behind, hadn't yet made the trek
for Peeps, fluorescent grass, hadn't rustled down the pig for Sunday brunch.

But soon the eggs hidden, the soccer ball basket, the bunny basket stuffed
inside a prickly bush, and soon enough they're running for the plastic lamb

barely resembling a lamb, for colors non-existent except at Wal-Mart,
soon enough all or nearly all, scooped up, added to the pile, and they're off

to the Salvation Army church, where the boy playing lead guitar
is cousin Carmen, the kid transformed to a turquoise-bunny-eared

rock star. *Through the veil of gloom and darkness / Where o death is now thy sting?*
Uncle Matt's triumphant percussion, Aunt Christi's booming, blessed soprano,

Rosie the soldier waving her hands, holding up God's ceiling, marching
as she sings. And then they're out of there, the kids with their bubble wands

and wind-up chicks, with their new, vague sense of a long haired, bearded,
sheet-swathed, half-naked guy encircled in beams of light and clouds,

the daughter trying out a *hallelujah* in the backseat scattered
with 250 million year old gastropod fossils now headed

for the sanctuary of the dirt road, for a forest resplendent
with mayapple, wake-robin, bloodroot, as the kids, itchy and hot,

too hot for clothes, peel them off, squeal through the just-leafed
dogwoods, hickories, sycamores, oaks, their voices lifting with each

squirrel, each unfurling fern. Full and hot, as if they'll never be hungry, never be cold again, as if this forest's party dress will never tatter;

biscuit-glutted, resurrection-drunk in the Oklahoma heat, cardinals exploding *Who-it? Who-it? Who-it?* Rosie cautioned not to heed

the anthems of the dead—Buddha, Allah, Krishna (*Ours is the only one who rose*), to stay for Bible Study, to trade in coos and croaks, buzzes

and chirps for Matthew 28, all the while every spring beauty, each poking-from-the-duff morel: *we're back, we're back; we've come back to life.*

ALL THINGS WANT TO FLOAT

When their strings finally snap, paper kites resist the urge
to land in wires, on roofs, in the tops of maples and oaks.

When spindles and whelks sway in the shallows,
they don't desire in the least to be picked up,

buffed, placed in rows beneath glass. In truth,
they'd prefer to flounder forever in the hissing tide.

Knowing full-well the science of sun and dew,
a spider casts her strand between two bushes.

When, at dawn, a human unwittingly passes through,
she dangles (cautiously, proudly) from her weightless arc

of stars. Cottonwood's fluff, thistle's pappus, lint confined
to the dryer: all long to hitch a ride to the Pinwheel Galaxy.

Not even a thing's heaviness exempts it, as logs,
tethered to flat-beds, unleash, sniff out fluid routes,

as boats, big as houses, loosen from moorings.
Good thing our brains are buoyant, bathed

in a cranial sea. Good thing, when at last we concede
to gravity, the scent of decay entices the swatted,

the often shooed away. Good thing, though preferring
to flit and bungle without us, they take us, hungrily, in.

MADE PURE BY HER INTERCESSION

Because no one could locate her file.
Because sometimes it was thick

like the abdomen of a moth, thin
like a golden-crowned kinglet's thin song.

Because, O gate of the saints, God elected her
with table divine. Because a stranger brought the key,

the path to the Tadpole Galaxy, a fire pit
of rain. Because the credenza was her pillar

of clouds, her stapler a star of the wave.
Because there was glitter, a Big Bang, a backward slant,

a blue dish blooming with soon-to-be-struck matches.
Because she wouldn't crawl through the big bay window

of bicker. O light of the grave! O hope of the guilty!
Even if she wasn't the brightest star

in Coma Berenices' wild hair cluster
she gulped down the welcome;

her brutal found a home on a diadem.

IT'S ALL GRAVY

a gravy with little brown specks
a gravy from the juices in a pan

the pan you could have dumped in the sink
now a carnival of flavor waiting to be scraped

loosened with splashes of milk of water of wine
let it cook let it thicken let it be spooned or poured

over bird over bovine over swine
the gravy of the cosmos bubbling

beside the resting now lifted to the table
gravy like an ongoing conversation

Uncle Benny's pork-pie hat
a child's peculiar way of saying *emergency*

seamlessly   with sides of potato of carrot of corn
seamlessly   while each door handle sings its own song

while giant cicadas ricochet off cycads and jellyfish sting
a gravy like the ether they swore the planets swam through

luminiferous   millions of times less dense than air
ubiquitous   impossible to define   a gravy like the God

Newton paid respect to when he argued
that to keep it all in balance to keep it from collapsing

to keep all the stars and planets from colliding
sometimes He had to intervene

a benevolent meddling like the hand
that stirs and stirs as the liquid steams
obvious and simple   everything and nothing
my gravy your gravy our gravy   the cosmological constant's

glutinous gravy   an iridescent and variably pulsing gravy
the gravy of implosion   a dying-that-births-dueodenoms gravy

gravy of doulas of dictionaries and of gold
the hand stirs   the liquid steams

and we heap the groaning platter with glistening
the celestial chef looking on as we lift our plates

lick them like a cat come back from a heavenly spin
because there is oxygen in our blood

because there is calcium in our bones
because all of us were cooked

in the gleaming Viking range
of the stars

Previous winners of the **saturnalia books poetry prize**:

Personification by Margaret Ronda
Winner of the Saturnalia Books Poetry Prize 2009
Selected by Carl Phillips

To the Bone by Sebastian Agudelo
Winner of the Saturnalia Books Poetry Prize 2008
Selected by Mark Doty

Famous Last Words by Catherine Pierce
Winner of the Saturnalia Books Poetry Prize 2007
Selected by John Yau

Dummy Fire by Sarah Vap
Winner of the Saturnalia Books Poetry Prize 2006
Selected by Forrest Gander

Correspondence by Kathleen Graber
Winner of the Saturnalia Books Poetry Prize 2005
Selected by Bob Hicok

The Babies by Sabrina Orah Mark
Winner of the Saturnalia Books Poetry Prize 2004
Selected by Jane Miller